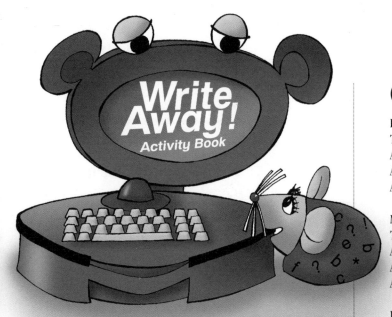

GW00599290

Introduction

This activity book accompanies **Write Away!** – a television series designed to provide models of writing for 7–9 year olds. It contains photocopiable activity sheets which promote writing and literacy skills, and offers suggestions for differentiated reading and writing extension activities. This material can be used either in follow-up work to the programmes or for independent classroom work.

The photocopiable pages are designed to be used by pupils of different levels of experience and can be adapted accordingly. The book covers a range of tasks involving text-, sentence- and word-level activities, from text analysis such as retelling a story, to use of speech bubbles and exploring elements of pattern in language. The teacher notes indicate the level of each of the tasks with the following icons:

Ⓣ text   Ⓢ sentence   Ⓦ word

A series of eight big-book-sized posters (available from Channel Four Learning) have been designed by PCET to complement the activities in this book. They provide an attractive teaching resource to stimulate and support children's understanding about writing.

Contents

Recipes for my Dad

1. Writing a recipe

(T)(S)(W) The children are asked to consider instructions in relation to running order. They distinguish between 'imperative' verbs and adverbs in the muddled-up cake recipe, write out the instructions in the correct order, and then write a recipe of their own. Here is the correct sequence:

- Weigh out the ingredients.
- Sieve the flour into the basin.
- Chop the fat and rub into the flour until it resembles fine breadcrumbs.
- Add the sugar.
- Slowly fold in the lightly beaten eggs.
- Spoon the mixture quickly into the greased tin.
- Bake in a moderate oven for 25 minutes.
- Eat it all up for tea!

To support the children in writing their own recipes, discuss the structure of a recipe (ingredients and method) and the type of language used, for example cooking verbs and the use of imperative verbs for giving instructions. Read aloud several recipes and encourage children to comment on the tense in which instructions are written (usually simple present). Talk about verbs and adverbs and ask the children to identify as many as possible.

Extension
(T) Ask the children to read each other's recipes and comment upon the accuracy and clarity of their written instructions.

Learning outcomes
- (T)(S) using bullet points, numbering and headings to give clarity to instructions
- (S) using the simple present tense
- (S)(W) identifying imperative verbs and their use as commands

2. How to ride a bicycle

(T)(S)(W) The children are asked to write instructions for riding a bicycle. They are given an annotated drawing of a bicycle to refer to for vocabulary, and sub-headings to help give a structure to their work.

(S) As a shared-writing activity, compose a range of instructions to highlight the tense used and the range and function of verbs related to the topic.

Extension
(T)(S) In pairs, ask children to read through each other's instructions and identify the sections that have the most clarity. Share these in a plenary session to discuss the most effective use of language, for example imperative verbs and mechanical devices such as headings and bullet points.

Learning outcomes
- (T) writing simple, clear instructions
- (S) using imperative verbs in a meaningful context
- (T)(S) using features of instructional texts such as sub-headings to clarify the instructions

3. My favourite game

(T)(S) The children are asked to choose their favourite game and brainstorm all the instructions that they can think of to explain how to play it. They should then number these in order of priority and write out the instructions in no more than 150 words.

(T)(S)(W) To support the activity, share a range of instructional texts with the children and consider illustrations and organisational devices such as numbering, and sub-headings. Remind them that instructions are written in the second person.

Extension
(T)(S) Ask the children to swap their instructions with a partner and then play the game following these instructions. As a result of their feedback to each other, the children could redraft their work using a word processor. A class book of games and how to play them could be compiled.

Learning outcomes
- (T)(W) collating relevant information by using key words and notes
- (T) writing clear instructions
- (T)(S) writing cohesive instructions with the use of organisational devices

Writing a recipe

 Read the instructions for making a cake. Underline the 'imperative' verbs in red and the adverbs in blue.

Chop the fat and rub into the flour until it resembles fine breadcrumbs.

Bake in a moderate oven for 25 minutes.

Spoon the mixture quickly into the greased tin.

Add the sugar.

Eat it all up for tea!

Slowly fold in the lightly beaten eggs.

Sieve the flour into the basin.

Weigh out the ingredients.

 These instructions are muddled up. Write them out in the correct order.

 On another sheet of paper, write out your own recipe for making a cheese sandwich.

Name...

How to ride a bicycle

 Write clear instructions for riding a bicycle.

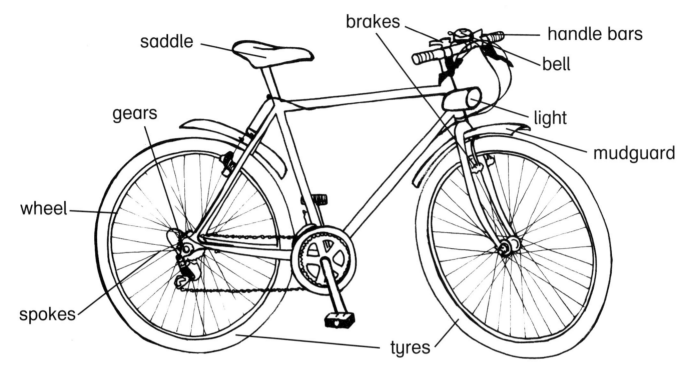

Use these points to help you:

How to get on a bike and balance.   How to make the bike move.

How to steer the bike.   How to stop.   How to stay safe on the bicycle.

....

....

....

....

....

....

....

....

My favourite game

What is your favourite game? Write down everything you can think of to explain how to play it.

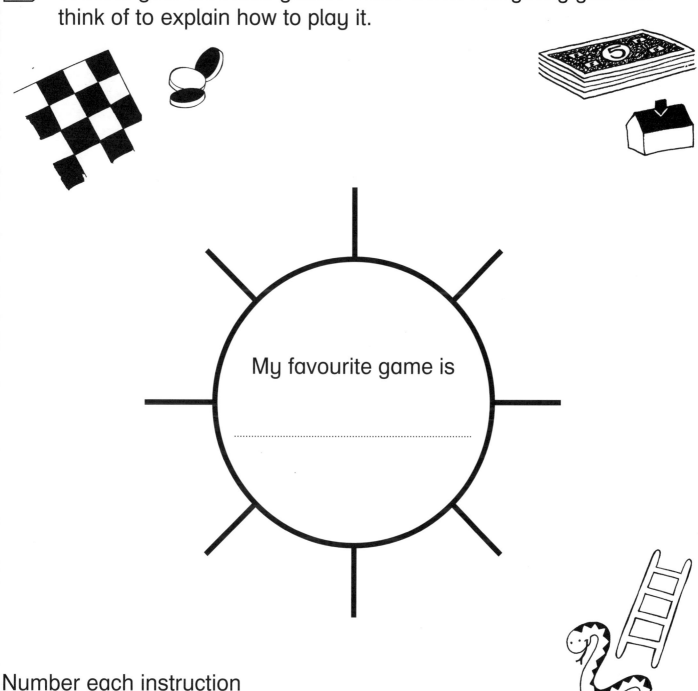

My favourite game is

....

Number each instruction in the right order.

On the back of this page, write a set of instructions for your favourite game in not more than 150 words. Use numbered points and pictures to help you.

Match Reporter

Two PCET posters are available for use in conjunction with these activities: one shows a sports report for a local paper and the other features a factual report on the hippopotamus.

1. Match report

(T)(S)(W) The children are asked to read the football report written by the journalist in the programme. They then use highlighter pens or crayons to underline the verbs and adjectives that describe the atmosphere and action of the game. Using a dictionary, they can look for synonyms that could be used to substitute the original words from the text.

As a shared-reading activity, children identify the use of 'powerful' adjectives and verbs in newspaper headlines and reports. Discuss the impact they have on the reader – can they predict the story from the headline? As a class, try substituting synonyms for key words in headlines and discuss any change they have on the meaning.

Extension
(T)(W) Ask children to write a new headline for the football report. Can they incorporate any of the synonyms they have found?

Learning outcomes
- (S)(W) identifying and using verbs and adjectives
- (T)(S) substituting adjectives and verbs and noting the effects on meaning
- (W) identifying synonyms and their use in improving the range of vocabulary used in writing

2. Read all about it!

(T)(S) The children are asked to look at a pictorial storyboard marked with different times of the day and dialogue in the form of speech bubbles. They then record the events on the storyboard in note form, and use the information to write a newspaper report.

Enlarge the activity sheet and go through the story with the children. Discuss the function of a newspaper report and the sorts of background information needed. Demonstrate the use of paragraphs to organise information. Remind children to write in the third person singular.

Extension activity
(T)(S) Working in pairs, ask the children to use the computer to edit each other's reports. They can make suggestions for possible deletions and word substitutions, paying attention to the effects these have on meaning. Then work together on layout and presentation.

Learning outcomes
- (T) making notes with a particular focus
- (T) writing a report
- (S) using paragraphs to organise writing

3. Writing from history

(T) The children are given a picture and a short passage to read about a Roman centurion. They are also given a planning sheet to help them to gather specific information in preparation for writing a report. Encourage them to write in note form.

(T) As a shared-reading and writing activity, select another information text and use a similar planning sheet to gather and sort key information that could be used for report writing. Focus on writing in note form, exploring the different ways of writing in shortened forms, and discuss the purpose of note-taking.

Extension
(T) The children can use their notes from the planning sheet as a basis for drafting a full report on Roman centurions, considering their audience as they write.

Learning outcomes
- (W) identifying key words or phrases from the children's reading to use in their writing
- (T) collecting and classifying information from a non-chronological report
- (T) understanding the function of note-making
- (T) using notes to organise and present information

Match report

FULHAM SET NEW RECORD AFTER BEATING CREWE

by Andy Sherwood

Fulham set a new club record after thumping Crewe 3-0. Goals from Geoff Horsefield, Barry Hayles and Kit Symons left manager Paul Bracewell celebrating. 'I wouldn't say it was easy – we got about the job and we did it well, and I'm very proud,' said Bracewell.

Horsefield started the celebrations when he drilled home a low shot from 10 yards after just 10 minutes. Barry Hayles then made it two, with a looping header from Lee Clark's cross, while Welsh defender, Kit Symons, made it 3-0 with a towering header from a Steve Haywood corner.

Crewe's closest chance came when Mark Feran hit the bar in the 32nd minute.

VICTORY TO UNITED YOUTH!!!!

by Rory Lewis

'Islington United Youth will win the league,' says the manager of the team after they won 3-2 against Highbury Youth.

It was an exciting game with lots of action. Kingsley scored a fantastic header. Goram passed a brilliant cross to Patrick who booted a pukka goal. But my favourite goal was by Ambrous when he blasted the ball into the back of the net!

Highbury Youth made a great effort with 2 goals scored by Smith and Allen.

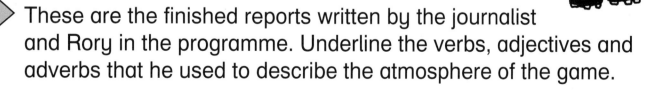

▷ These are the finished reports written by the journalist and Rory in the programme. Underline the verbs, adjectives and adverbs that he used to describe the atmosphere of the game.

▷ Collect synonyms for these words.

▷ Try putting the synonyms in place of the original words. Do they make sense?

Read all about it!

 Study the pictures below. Make notes on what you see happening. Comment on:

- where the events took place
- who was involved
- when it happened
- the things people said
- the order that things happened
- how things ended up

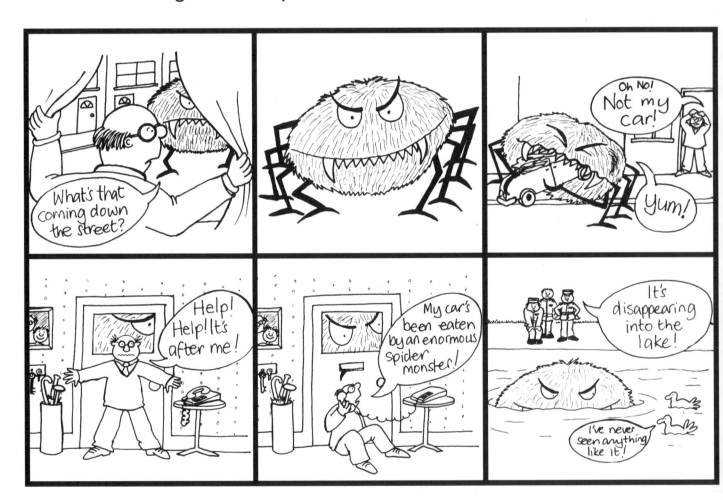

 On the back of this sheet of paper, write a newspaper report describing the events at No.5 The Street in not more than 120 words. Try to use adjectives and verbs that will make your story more exciting. Organise your writing into paragraphs and remember that the person reading the report will not see the pictures.

Writing from history

A centurion

Between 31bc and ad476, the Romans conquered lands all over the world, including Britain. They needed massive armies to defend these places. To become a soldier in the Roman army, young men had to be: born in Rome, tall, brave, healthy, ready to travel and able to read and write. To become strong and learn discipline, new soldiers built roads along which the legions of troops could travel. They learnt to march carrying heavy backpacks and to fight by attacking their prisoners. The best soldiers became centurions, who each commanded one hundred soldiers. They had to be excellent fighters, brave and ruthless. To protect their camps from intruders a new password was given to the centurions each day. The centurions were very highly paid.

 Use this planning sheet to collect and sort the facts in the passage above about a Roman centurion. Write the information in note form.

Who they were and why they were called centurions:	Where and when they lived:
• .... • .... • .... •	• .... • .... • .... • ....
What they wore and how they lived:	What they did as centurions:
• .... • .... • .... •	• .... • .... • .... • ....

Daniella's Diary

A PCET poster featuring diary writing is available for use in conjunction with these activities.

1. A day in the life of...

(T) The children are asked to write a diary entry as if they too had met Jacqueline Wilson on a boat trip along the river Thames. They are encouraged to record their thoughts and feelings as if the diary were their best friend.

(T) As a stimulus for diary writing, ask the children to recall their first day in class or at school. Can they remember how they felt and describe what happened on that day? Did they know any other children beforehand, were they worried about being in a new place and meeting new people? What other concerns were there? Explore these thoughts and feelings in shared writing.

Extension

(T) Working with a writing partner, children can select one element of diary writing such as character description or setting, and use it as a basis for an imaginative piece of writing.

Learning outcomes

- (T) using a diary as an *aide-mémoire* to writing
- (T)(S)(W) describing experiences and settings effectively
- (T) developing note-taking in a purposeful context

2. I didn't imagine this, it really happened

(T)(W) The children are invited to draw upon all their sensory experiences to reflect on an everyday event in their lives. Headings are used to invite these responses, and children are asked to consider the quality of vocabulary they use in their descriptions.

(T)(S) Read extracts from well-known diaries such as those mentioned in the programme, for example Samuel Pepys. Discuss the use of writing in the first person singular and the tense used by the diarist. Use shared writing to model diary writing reflecting these conventions.

Extension

(T)(S) Children can use the same format to write an imaginary diary of a child living in another time such as during the great fire of London, or a time in the future.

Learning outcomes

- (S) distinguishing the features of writing in the first person singular
- (T)(S)(W) collecting material suitable for creating moods and setting scenes in imaginative writing
- (S) using the past tense with consistency

3. Secret diary

(T) Here children make a mini-diary following the instructions on the activity sheet. They then use this to keep a diary over the school week. Suggest that conventional entries are not necessary and that children might simply record a smell, an idea or a thought. The space provided is limited, so this will require children to be concise in their composition. Discuss the following points with the children:

- Remember that a diary is private – they can write whatever they want to write.
- They don't have to write down everything that they do.
- They can write in note form – using dashes, commas, diagrams and pictures to help them to remember things.
- They can use ideas from their diary for writing stories later.

Extension

(T) Develop the habit of diary writing in the form of, for example, a school journal where children are free to comment on a social and academic event each day.

Learning outcomes

- (T) exploring ways of writing ideas in a shortened form
- (T) identifying purposes of making notes
- (T) editing text to fit a particular space

Name..

A day in the life of...

Imagine that you met Jacqueline Wilson on the river boat today instead of Daniella.

 Write about your meeting and the trip in diary form.

Before you write, think about:
- a name for your diary
- how you felt about meeting a famous author
- your first impressions of her (did she look or sound as you had imagined that she would?)
- how you felt about television cameras and crew watching you
- good and bad memories of the day

Remember:
- where you went
- what you saw and heard
- you can write in note form if you want
- Jacqueline Wilson and the television crew aren't going to read this so you can be honest!

Dear ....

9.00 a.m. ....

10.00 ....

11.00 ....

12.00 ....

1.00 p.m. ....

2.00 ....

3.00 ....

4.00 ....

5.00 ....

6.00 ....

I didn't imagine this, it really happened

Diaries can help remind us of good and bad times in our lives. They can also be a great way of collecting ideas for writing stories and reports at a later date.

> Use these boxes to help you remember and then describe one of the different things that has happened to you this week, such as falling out with a friend, playing a good game, or being late for school.

When did it happen?	What did you hear?
Where did it happen?	What did you smell?
Why did it happen?	How did you feel?
What did you see?	What did you do?

> On the back of this sheet, describe what happened using the most interesting and imaginative words that you can.

Secret diary

 Make your own mini-diary using the template below. Follow these instructions:

1. Fold paper in half lengthways and then into quarters.

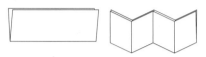

2. Open out then fold it in half widthways. Cut along the dotted line on the central fold.

3. Open it out again. Cut along small dotted lines marked inside.

4. Fold paper in half lengthways. Push inwards to make a book, holding the two outside quarters.

5. Flatten the box. Bend flap around the outside covers. Fasten your diary up.

Write one diary entry for each of the next five days at school. Keep your entries brief.

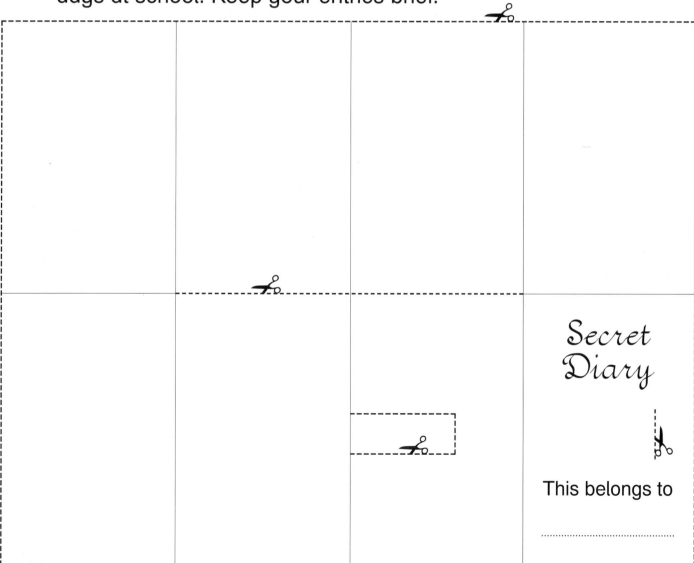

Secret Diary

This belongs to

....

With Love From Merrylegs

A PCET poster featuring a letter to a local newspaper is available for use in conjunction with these activities.

1. The art of persuasion

(T)(S) The children are given a framework for designing a poster persuading their peers to get fit. Help them to focus on the content of their argument – why, for instance, is it important to be fit? Then discuss how to use an opening statement, supporting arguments and a concluding statement. Compare and evaluate the strength of each other's argument. Discuss the process of persuasion and how children use their skills of persuasion to get something they want from their parents and friends. Encourage children to identify and utilise these in written form. You may want to give examples for each:

Opening statements:

Legs are made for walking – walk don't ride to school.

Crunch a carrot not a crisp.

Don't be a couch potato.

Don't pig out, work out.

Supporting arguments:

Feel good, look good.

Unhealthy kids make unhealthy adults.

(T)(S)(W) As a shared-writing activity, discuss how information is presented, for example through wordplay, alliteration, jingles, and the impact it has on the intended audience.

Extension

(T)(W) Use the children's designs to create computer-generated posters. Work in groups to launch a 'get fit' campaign throughout the school, focusing on the different methods of persuasion.

Learning outcomes

- (S) using imperative verbs to make powerful statements
- (T) assembling and sequencing points of view in a logical order
- (W) designing a poster

2. What I really, really want!

(T) The children are asked to think of something that they really want, to make a list of statements about why they want it and to put these in order of priority. They are then asked to write arguments in support of their statements.

(S) As a shared-writing activity, help the children to develop the use of connectives such as adverbs, phrases and conjunctions to structure their argument, for example: 'If only I had a PlayStation then my handwriting would be better.'

Extension

(T)(S)(W) Ask children to select their strongest statements and arguments to use in a letter to their parents. Encourage them to consider their use of vocabulary and a style that is most likely to interest the reader, gain their sympathy and persuade them.

Learning outcomes

- (T)(S) ordering points to support an argument
- (T)(W) presenting a point of view in writing
- (S) using connectives for structuring arguments

I need the exercise.

3. Support your cause

(T)(S)(W) The children are asked to choose one of the topics on the activity sheet that they feel strongly about and use a writing frame to structure and organise a persuasive piece of writing. Emphasis is given to statements, arguments and summary.

Share with children persuasive texts such as topical letters to the press and newspaper articles that deal with issues pertinent to the children's interests, for example animal welfare or the local environment. As a shared-reading activity, highlight key elements of the texts, how information is presented, how points are linked together, different styles chosen for the audience and the types of language used.

Extension

(T)(S) Working with a writing partner, ask the children to edit and strengthen their writing to make it have a greater impact on the reader. Consider the use of phrases such as: 'You will find that...'; 'It could affect your life through...'; or 'You must agree that...' which will encourage the reader to agree.

Learning outcomes

- (T)(S) using linguistic devices for persuasion
- (S) linking points persuasively
- (T)(S) presenting and sequencing logical argument
- (T) summarising key points

The art of persuasion

 Design a poster to persuade your friends to get fit.

In box ⓐ Tell them what you think they should do.

ⓐ

In box ⓑ Give them reasons why being fit and healthy is good. Make up your own arguments.

ⓑ

In box ⓒ Remind them again about what they should do to get fit.

ⓒ

Name...

What I really, really want!

Think about how you could persuade your mum or dad to let you have something that you really want. It might be for example a new bike, a PlayStation or a pet.

▷ Make statements about why you want it, then number your statements in order of importance.

I need a .... because ....

....

If I had a .... it would ....

....

I could ....

if I had a ....

I'm a lonely child.

I need a dog because...

I need the exercise.

It'll frighten burglars.

It will chase cats.

▷ Write down further arguments to support your statements.

It will improve my ....

....

It will help me to ....

....

It will make you ....

....

Support your cause

Do you feel strongly about any of these issues?

the amount of homework you're given

school uniforms

the cost of football kits

dogs fouling the pavements

cruelty to animals

Choose one of these topics. Use this writing frame to organise your opinions and facts to help you to persuade other people to understand your point of view.

Make an opening statement which outlines your point of view.

I feel strongly about .... because ....

....

Give reasons why you feel strongly about this issue, using any information you have to back up your arguments.

The reason I feel like this is ....

....

Give an example of how the reader can be affected by this issue.

You will find that ....

could affect your life through ....

Make a concluding statement that sums up and strengthens your argument.

The facts that I have given show that ....

....

Now read this to your partner. How do they respond?

Your Zoo Needs You!

A PCET poster demonstrating how to design a poster advertisement is available for use in conjunction with these activities.

1. Tag lines

(T)(W) The children are asked to compose tag lines to accompany poster illustrations. The subject for the poster is outlined under each illustration. Encourage the children to make a play on words.

Collect tag lines from commercial posters and advertisements in magazines in order to discuss play on words, and so on. Make a list of proverbs and sayings that children know and explore how they may be used for tag lines. As shared writing, compose some tag lines using some of the suggestions on the activity sheet.

Extension

(T)(W) Share the tag lines in a plenary session to discuss the range of linguistic devices used and which tag line they think most effective and why.

Learning outcomes

*   (W) using alliteration/ homonyms/ rhyme
*   (T) using persuasive writing
*   (W) using linguistic devices to appeal to an audience

2. Copy and layout

(T) Several versions of illustrations and copy about puppy training are printed on the sheet. The children are asked to cut these out and experiment with the selection given, choosing certain items and arranging them to create an attractive poster with impact.

Discuss the composition of posters and focus on the text copy (apart from the tag line) that gives information such as: date, time, venues of a performance or the brand and availability of a product, and so on. Collect a selection of posters and advertisements and encourage children to identify the tag line and copy. Encourage them to think about the decisions that have to be made about the layout of illustration and text.

Extension

(T)(S) Ask the children to consider information they may want to include on the poster such as who is running the class and their qualifications, the age of the puppies, and so on. Using ICT, ask the children to compose a tag line considering the impact of design: size and type of font layout and position on the poster.

Learning outcomes

*   (T)(S) using a range of presentation skills
*   (T) comparing the way information is presented
*   (T) understanding the impact of presentation on targeted audience

3. Pantomime poster

(T)(S)(W) The children are asked to design a poster for a school pantomime. Suggestions are made to help them consider how to incorporate all the elements of copy, tag line and illustration and to make it eye-catching and appealing to the reader.

Encourage the children to study advertisements and layouts of other posters. Discuss the appeal of the illustrations and tag line, the type of information given in the copy, and how size and type of font is designed to guide the reader. Talk about the need for a concise and appealing message, the importance of presentation and the use of carefully checked spellings and punctuation.

Extension

(T)(S) Use ICT to make a published version of the poster, trying out various layouts and a range of fonts and types of print, selecting the most appropriate for the final version.

Learning outcomes

*   (T) writing concisely
*   (T)(S) using a range of presentation skills
*   (T) using ICT to bring a poster to a published form
*   (S)(W) checking for correct punctuation and spelling

School Pantomime

Tag lines

 Compose a tag line for each of these posters. How can you make it fun to read?

Think about using one or more of these ideas:
- a saying or proverb
- alliteration
- rhyming words
- homonyms

Write a tag line reminding drivers to slow down.

Write a tag line to make people want to buy this toothpaste.

Copy and layout

Carefully cut out the illustrations and the copy. Using a sheet of A4 paper, experiment with layout to produce a poster for puppy-training classes. Paste up the version you find the most appealing and colour it in.

Puppy Training Classes

Wednesdays 7.30 p.m. March and April
At the Church Hall, Silk Lane, Cobham

Puppy Training Classes

Wednesdays 7.30 p.m. March and April
At the Church Hall, Silk Lane, Cobham

Puppy Training Classes

Wednesdays 7.30 p.m. March and April
At the Church Hall, Silk Lane, Cobham

Puppy
Training Classes

Wednesdays 7.30 p.m. March and April
At the Church Hall, Silk Lane, Cobham

Name..

Pantomime poster

 Design a poster to advertise a school pantomime. Consider:

the copy	the tag line	layout	illustration
• title of show • date and time of performances • venue	• snappy and fun • make people want to see the pantomime	• where to place copy and tag line • size and type of print • use of illustration	• appeal and impact of illustration • how it enhances text size and placement

A Song for Summer

1. Clapping the rhythm

(T)(S) Children are asked to clap and count the syllables in each line of the nursery rhyme Humpty Dumpty and underline words that rhyme. Using the information they have gathered they are asked to write a second verse.

(T) Gather all the verses together to make a class book to develop a ballad telling the story of what happened to Humpty Dumpty.

Model this activity using other well-known nursery rhymes, songs or playground chants to:

> (T)(W) clap out the rhythm
>
> (W) identify rhyming words
>
> (S) reinforce the use of capital letters at the beginning of each line
>
> (S) notice the use of commas at the end of lines in songs and poems and where full stops occur.

Extension

(T) Children can compose a chorus to go between each verse. This can be modelled through a shared-writing activity.

Learning outcomes

- (W) revisiting syllables as a tool for songwriting
- (W) recognising which words rhyme and differences in spelling
- (S) using capital letters and commas for songwriting format
- (W) clapping out and counting syllables

2. Jumbled mumbles

(T) The lyrics for Hannah's summer song are jumbled up. The children are asked to cut out each line and paste in the correct order, paying attention to verses and chorus.

Familiarise children with the terms 'verse' and 'chorus' using pop songs as examples. As a shared singing activity, go through 'A Song for Summer' before and after the activity as preparation and for self-correction.

Extension

(T)(W) This activity can be made more challenging by cutting up the verses line by line and re-ordering them.

Learning outcomes

- (T) understanding the terms 'verse' and 'chorus'
- (T)(W) understanding of rhyme through sequencing of lyrics
- (T) using contextual cues to help with meaning of lyrics

3. Winter words

(T)(W) Using Hannah's song as a model, the children work in pairs to compose new lyrics for one verse of a wintertime song, to be sung to the same tune as 'A Song for Summer'. The children are asked to brainstorm a list of wintry words and use them to explore a range of words that rhyme.

Discuss the different themes in the song and brainstorm themes suitable to write about for winter.

Extension

(T) As a class activity, select the best verses and as shared writing compose a winter chorus. Rehearse and perform the finished song.

Learning outcomes

- (T) generating ideas relevant to a topic
- (W) discussing choice of words and phrases
- (T) writing new or extended verses based on models of performance

Clapping the rhythm

When songs and poems rhyme we can remember the words more easily. Do you know this nursery rhyme?

☐ Humpty Dumpty sat on the wall,

☐ Humpty Dumpty had a great fall,

☐ All the king's horses and all the king's men,

☐ Couldn't put Humpty together again.

 Clap the rhythm.
1. How many syllables can you count in each line? Write the number in each box.
2. Underline all the rhyming words.

 Write a second verse for the nursery rhyme. Try to make each line have the same number of syllables as the first verse.

Verse Two

Humpty Dumpty...

....

....

....

....

Jumbled mumbles

This is the summertime song that Hannah composed, but it is muddled up.

 Unjumble and cut out the verses, and then paste them in the right order.

One, two, three, four,
Sun, sand, sea and more!

Summer, summer, summer, summer, summertime,
Everybody's happy, everybody's fine.
Summer, summer, summer, summer, summertime,
If you like the summer you're a friend of mine.

Surfing over enormous waves,
Exploring dark and spooky caves,
Leaving footprints in soft, wet sand,
As we go walking hand in hand.

Crabs in my bucket, shrimps in my net,
Happy here as long as they're wet.
Looking in rock pools, finding shells,
Listening to the story the seagull tells.

One, two, three, four,
Sun, sand, sea and more!

Summer, summer, summer, summer, summertime,
Everybody's happy, everybody's fine.
Summer, summer, summer, summer, summertime,
If you like the summer you're a friend of mine.

Think of ice creams, think of sun,
Think of the seaside, it's number one!
Sky is sunny, sea is blue,
I'm having fun, hope you are too!

Check to make sure the verses and choruses are in the right order before you stick them down. Singing it through might help.

Winter words

These are the words for one verse from Hannah's summertime song.
Watch the programme again to remind you of the tune.

Surfing over enormous waves,
Exploring dark and spooky caves,
Leaving footprints in soft, wet sand,
As we go walking hand in hand.

▷ Work with a partner and write a verse for a wintertime song. Use the same tune as 'A Song for Summer'.

....

....

....

....

Brainstorm some wintry words	Think of some good rhyming words
cold ⟶	bold, sold
snow ⟶	blow, glow, toe

Who is Stereo Steve?

A PCET poster featuring a character description is available for use in conjunction with these activities.

1. Mugshots

Ⓢ Ⓦ The children are asked to draw appropriate expressions on a sheet of paper containing six blank faces labelled with different moods. They then use a dictionary to find more adjectives to describe their completed faces.

As a class, model the activity by drawing a blank face and selecting a word such as 'naughty', then invite different children to draw a feature on the face following the descriptive instructions given by the rest of the class. Brainstorm a range of words associated with, for example, a 'naughty' character such as Dennis the Menace.

Extension

Ⓣ Children could select their favourite face and write about the circumstances that caused their character's mood.

Learning outcomes

- Ⓣ making notes in preparation for a character study
- Ⓢ Ⓦ collecting adjectives and verbs to describe a character
- Ⓣ writing about one aspect of a character

2. Here is Stereo Steve

Ⓣ Ⓦ The activity sheet contains an annotated picture of Stereo Steve describing his appearance and elements of his behaviour, his likes and his dislikes. Using this as a model, children are asked to design their own cartoon character and make similar annotations around their drawing.

Ⓣ Enlarge the annotated drawing of Stereo Steve and, as a class, discuss how the combination of drawings and notes can be used for planning and, in this case, developing the detail of a character to inform story writing. Revise note-making by commenting on examples offered.

Extension

Ⓣ Children can design a storyboard that features their character, considering appropriate settings, plot and other characters to complement the main one.

Learning outcomes

- Ⓣ using annotated drawings to plan story writing
- Ⓣ writing a character sketch focusing on details of appearance and behaviour
- Ⓣ revising and extending work on making notes

3. Storyboard from scratch

Ⓣ The children are asked to plan their own stories considering character, setting and plot and write their ideas on a blank storyboard with six frames.

Ⓣ Ⓢ As a class activity, ask the children to work in pairs to read a range of comics. Ask them to comment on devices used to depict, for example, naughty characters, speed or the passage of time, how dialogue is written and the interplay between the illustrations and narrative text. Ask them to give examples of where the reader is left to fill in the gaps, for example what is drawn and written and what is left to the reader's imagination?

Extension

Ⓣ Ⓢ Once the children have planned their storyboard, they could use ICT to add the dialogue and narrative texts and publish their comic strips in a class anthology.

Learning outcomes

- Ⓣ using a storyboard to plan a story
- Ⓣ Ⓢ making use of their knowledge of the cartoon genre in their own writing
- Ⓣ developing use of settings

Mugshots

 Put different expressions on these faces.

happy

surprised

angry

sneaky

asleep

miserable

Underneath each face, write similar adjectives that describe the mood of the person you have drawn. Use a dictionary to help you.

Here is Stereo Steve

Here is Stereo Steve.

He's called Stereo Steve because he wears headphones all the time.

He wears cool clothes.

He gets words mixed up because he's always playing his stereo.

He doesn't walk, he jives.

He likes football.

He can't hear what people say because of his headphones.

The stereo plays funky music all the time.

He's full of mischief.

 Now design your own comic strip character. Make notes to describe:

- what he or she looks like
- what clothes they wear
- what they like and dislike doing
- their behaviour
- their character

- what is special about them, for example, Stereo Steve's headphones and Dennis the Menace's stripy jumper

Storyboard from scratch

 Use this storyboard to plan a comic strip. Think about:

- where the story takes place
- the characters involved
- the characters' behaviour
- what they say
- what happens

It was a Dark and Lonely Night...

A PCET poster relating to place and setting, comparing different styles of writing, is available for use in conjunction with these activities.

1. What if...?

(T)(W) The children are asked to exercise their imaginations by completing the 'What if...?' questions in an attempt to make everyday objects appear extraordinary. They then draft an opening paragraph that sets the scene for a story.

Encourage the children to come up with interesting adjectives to describe the shape, texture, colour and size of everyday objects. Discuss the notion of paragraphs and how the opening paragraph needs to set the scene for the rest of the story leaving the reader wanting to read on.

Extension

(T)(W) Talk about other ways of describing things such as the use of imagery by incorporating simile or metaphor into their writing. Give examples of these such as: 'eyes as green as the sea'; 'claw-like fingers'; or 'teeth as sharp as knives'. At a plenary session, invite the children to read aloud their opening paragraphs. Which were the most appealing and why?

Learning outcomes

- (T) organising a story into paragraphs
- (T) developing the use of settings for stories
- (S)(W) understanding the function and effect of adjectives
- (T) writing openings to create suspense, build tension, and set scenes

2. Selecting adjectives and adverbs

(T)(S)(W) The children are asked to insert adjectives and adverbs into the gaps in a short passage. The choice of words should give impact to the story paragraph. They then need to identify which are adjectives and which are verbs and write them in the correct column on the chart.

Discuss the role of adjectives and adverbs in descriptive writing and how adjectives qualify nouns and adverbs qualify verbs. Discuss the use of the suffix 'ly' for identifying adverbs. Encourage children to experiment with different words to see how they impact on the noun or verb they qualify before settling on their final choice.

Extension

(T)(S) At a plenary session, share the range of words the children have chosen. How has the choice of words influenced the mood of the story? Which words are the most powerful? Can the words be classified into categories? Use a category such as speed to compile lists of alternative words for future writing, for example the knight galloped... steadily, furiously, hastily, and so on.

Learning outcomes

- (S)(W) identifying and understanding the function and effect of adjectives and adverbs
- (S) understanding the impact of adjectives and adverbs through cloze procedure
- (S) using adverbs and adjectives with greater discrimination in writing
- (T) writing own examples of descriptive language

3. Opening paragraphs

(T)(S) The children are asked to complete the opening paragraphs of stories from different genres using the notes to help them. They should consider how to continue setting the scene using appropriate descriptive language.

Provide a collection of books representing different genres. Talk about the sort of language that occurs in stories of a particular genre. Discuss with the children how they decide what sort of story the opening phrases on the activity sheet represent.

Extension

(T) Ask the children to make a collection of opening phrases to help them with their story writing. Sort them by genre.

Learning outcomes

- (T) developing settings for a specific genre
- (S)(W) understanding the function of adjectives and adverbs and how they impact on the story
- (T) investigating and collecting opening phrases
- (T) writing independently

What if...?

Jamie, the scriptwriter, uses these examples to show how imagination can change the ordinary into the extraordinary:

 A drinks can feels cold and metallic...What if it was suddenly squidgy or furry?

 A sweet is smooth and sweet...What if it was suddenly hot and bitter?

▷ Finish these:

A table feels smooth and flat... What if it was suddenly ....
.... ?

A glass is transparent and fragile... What if it was suddenly ....
.... ?

A pillow is soft and light... What if it was suddenly ....
.... ?

A piece of paper is blank and empty... What if it was suddenly ....
.... ?

A mirror reflects... What if it was suddenly ....
.... ?

▷ Write three more of your own.

....

....

....

▷ Now choose one of the 'What if...' ideas to help you write an opening paragraph to set the scene for a story. Remember to finish the paragraph on an exciting note, such as: 'I felt a cold hand on my shoulder...'

Selecting adjectives and adverbs

beautiful	dangerous	terrible	quickly	brave	ugly	trusting
horrible	thick	carefully	safe	cool	strong	wicked	proud

▷ Fill in the spaces to make this story more exciting. Use these adjectives and adverbs to help you, or find some of your own.

With no thought to the danger, the .... knight galloped

.... across the blazing field. The air was filled with the

.... smell of fire and .... smoke stung his nose

and throat. The .... flames licked at the legs of Shadow,

his .... horse. She was terrified of the fire but she held up

her .... head knowing that Godwin would lead her to

safety. He searched for .... patches of

ground where the fire had not got its hold.

Through the corner of his eye he caught sight

of water and steered Shadow ....

towards it, hoping that .... water would

shield them from the heat.

▷ Now sort the words you have chosen into the right columns.

Adjectives	Adverbs

Opening paragraphs

 These are the opening words from different types of stories. Think about what type of story each one might be and continue the paragraphs.

Consider:
• using interesting words such as adjectives and adverbs to give impact
• making everyday things extraordinary
• creating an exciting finish to the paragraph

The trees of the dark, dark forest loomed menacingly above

Selina as she ....

....

....

....

Spacecraft 010 crashed with a menacing thud on the pink planet

....

....

....

....

Once there was a golden frog who..

....

....

....

....

Beginnings, Middles and Endings

A PCET poster demonstrating how to write dialogue is available for use in conjunction with these activities.

1. Cinders 2

(T) Children are asked to read this imagined sequel to the Cinderella story to identify the beginning, middle and ending, explore how they are used for plot development and rewrite the story putting it into paragraphs.

Discuss with the class how the story opens on a high point and how the reader is drawn into the story through the device of high and low points. Discuss how, as one dilemma is overcome, another is presented, and that the skill of the writer is the use of cliffhangers to engage the reader's curiosity until a conclusion is met. The concluding paragraph can, however, present the reader with an unexpected twist.

Extension

(T) Invite the children to consider the use of high and low points in stories to plan an extension to the story so far or a sequel to another traditional tale they know. They can plan their story as a list, map, notes, diagram or simple storyboard. Once satisfied with the plans, they can use them to write an illustrated version of their story.

Learning outcomes
*   (T) exploring dilemmas in a story
*   (T) writing alternatives/ sequels to known stories
*   (T) planning and identifying the stages of a story
*   (T) writing independently
*   (T) plotting a sequence of episodes

2. Cinderella characters

(T) This activity explores how events can raise an issue or dilemma and shape character development. In the version of the Cinderella story on the activity sheet, the children are given some key events in the story and then asked to identify how this affects the character.

(T) Read the class the original story of Cinderella and together list the features of the central characters. How do they know about each one? Through discussion, help the children to identify the events that lead them to make judgements about a character, for example that the ugly sisters are mean. And what factors make them sympathise with Cinderella?

Extension

(T) Ask the children to either make a labelled diagram of one of the characters in this story or write a letter to their best friend telling them all about the character.

Learning outcomes
*   (T) understanding how alternative versions can change character perception
*   (T) writing character sketches
*   (T) understanding how one function of story text is to describe characters and their interaction with events and other characters

3. Science-fiction Cinderella

(T)(S)(W) The children are presented with a story framework. Each section commences with an introductory phrase. Using this framework, the children are asked to complete the story.

Read through the phrases together and ask the children to suggest the genre. Relate the discussion to media and book texts they know of a similar genre; story structure; beginnings, middles and endings; the use of high and low points to create tension, suspense and mood; and possibilities of character development through events. Discuss previous work on the way that adjectives and adverbs can create atmosphere.

Extension

(T) Using the writing framework as an example, ask children to choose their favourite genre and design a similar writing frame for their writing partner to complete, concentrating on the beginning, middle and ending of the story.

Learning outcomes
*   (T) identifing the stages of a story
*   (T) sequencing a story
*   (T)(S)(W) understanding of genre to determine language use, settings and character development

Cinders 2

Once upon a time, Cinders and Prince Charming were very, very happy. Their favourite place in the whole world was the banqueting room on the second floor of their castle. They had all their meals there. The only bad thing was that it was such a long way from one end of the table to the other, that they sometimes had to shout to make themselves heard. Meanwhile the ugly sisters were very, very cross at being cheated by their sister. They set off for Prince Charming's castle with a secret plan. Pretending that their mother had died and that they were homeless, they would trick Prince Charming into divorcing Cinderella and making them joint queens. Much to Cinderella's annoyance, Prince Charming opened the door to her sisters. Once inside, the ugly sisters persuaded Prince Charming to give them the run of the castle. Prince Charming was completely taken by their flattering ways and Cinders was made to be a servant again. They persuaded the Prince to let them polish his treasure, count his money and sign some official forms. One of these is a paper saying that the Prince will divorce Cinders because she is unkind to her sisters. Cinders and Prince Charming have a terrible row. The Ugly Sisters steal up behind her and tie Cinderella up. They imprison her and force her to sleep under the table, like a dog. Hearing of their cruel treatment and realising how much he loves Cinderella, the Prince decides to rescue her. Meanwhile, the sisters put Cinders on trial. Prince Charming enters as his ex-wife is sentenced to execution. It all goes horribly wrong as Cinders ends up tying them all up and walking out, leaving her ex-husband to marry her Ugly Sisters after all!

▷ Write this story out and put it into paragraphs.

Cinderella characters

 What do these events tell you about the characters in 'Cinders 2'? Fill in the characteristics column. The first one is done for you.

Events		Characteristics
	• She tells the prince not to answer the door. • She calls the prince a birdbrain and goes for him with a broom after he tells the sisters where the treasure is.	• She doesn't like her sisters as she knows they are up to no good and will only cause trouble.
	• He lets the sisters into the castle. • He tells Cinderella that he's the boss and that she is only jealous of the sisters. • He decides to rescue Cinderella.	
	• They pretend their mother is dead and that they are homeless. • They cry for help outside the door. • They hold a trial for Cinderella and pronounce judgment.	

Science-fiction Cinderella

> Use this framework to help you
> create a science-fiction story.

Cinderella opened the door of her space capsule only to find ....
....
....

Behind her she heard a soft scrunching noise that made her spine tingle
....
....

Thankfully ....
....
....

t only now remained for her to ....
....
....

At last ....
....
....

Amber's Play

1. Setting the scene

(T)(S) The children are asked to use the story of Goldilocks and the Three Bears as a basis for planning a play in six scenes. Suggestions for setting each scene are given and Scene 1 is described in detail as an example.

As a shared-text activity, carefully consider the layout of a playscript and identify key features in terms of scene setting. Discuss the functions of this device:

- to inform actors of their environment
- to give them clues about how to behave and react
- to give information to a director
- to help create mood and atmosphere

Explore the activity sheet to ensure that children understand what to do and to remind children that the scene-setting is written in the present tense.

Learning outcomes
- (S) writing using the present tense
- (T)(S)(W) creating moods and setting scenes for a playscript
- (T) focusing on setting scenes to create suspense and build tension
- (T) writing a playscript using a known story

Extension
(S)(W) Children can think up and devise sound effects for their scenes such as the rustling of leaves, the hooting of an owl, and so on. Discuss the need for abbreviation in stage directions such as SFX for sound effects and the use of adjectives and adverbs to succinctly describe sound.

2. Stage directions

(T)(S)(W) The children are asked to write the stage directions for each scene in the story of Goldilocks and the Three Bears. Explain to them that stage directions enable the director to tell the actors how to behave.

Discuss the activity sheet and the example given. Talk about detailing the actions and the use of interesting verbs and adverbs to help the actors decide on, for example, how to move. Discuss the use of present tense when writing. Refer to the Gingerbread Man, the play in the programme, as a way of discussing the function of stage directions – how did the actors know to creep around and bump into each other?

Extension
(T)(W) Give stage directions for Goldilock's behaviour when she gets home and is confronted by her mother.

Learning outcomes
- (T) writing independently
- (T) writing simple, clear instructions for actors to follow
- (T) sequencing events
- (S) writing using the present tense
- (T) writing a playscript using a known story

Setting the scene

Use the story of Goldilocks and the Three Bears as a basis for planning a play. Describe what you would see in the six scenes in the play. Scene 1 has been done for you.

Scene 1 **In the depths of an eerie forest.** Owls are heard hooting and branches reach out to grab Goldilocks. No path can be seen. In the distance there is some smoke coming from a chimney.	**Scene 2** **Outside the bear's cottage.**
Scene 3 **Inside the kitchen/lounge.**	**Scene 4** **Inside the bedroom.** 
Scene 5 **Inside the kitchen.**	**Scene 6** **Inside the bedroom.**

Stage directions

Lots of things happen in a play, so the actors have to be told what to do.
Imagine the scene in the three bears' cottage after Goldilocks has come in.

 Write down in sequence everything she does.
The first part is done for you.

In the three bears' kitchen

Goldilocks sniffs the air and smells
porridge. She looks at the table centre
stage and hungrily walks to the big
bowl, rubbing her tummy and licking
her lips. She peers into the big bowl
and greedily takes a mouthful of
porridge. Goldilocks...

In the three bears' lounge

....

....

....

....

In the three bears' bedroom

....

....

....

....

....